HYPNOTISM SIMPLIFIED

A Practical and Easy Guide to Mesmerism

By

STEPHEN MARTIN

This explains in simple language just what
Hypnotism and Mesmerism are; how to
mesmerise and hypnotise; the various
wonderful results which may be obtained from
both; how to use hypnotism safely; and, finally,
it gives directions for the use of hypnotism as
applied to oneself to strengthen the will and
attain one's desires.

HYPNOTISM SIMPLIFIED
A PRACTICAL AND EASY GUIDE TO MESMERISM

BY

STEPHEN MARTIN

First published November 1916

TABLE OF CONTENTS

PREFACE

IF any excuse were needed for another book on the subject of Hypnotism and Mesmerism the best, perhaps, that could be urged would be the one of price. Although there are many books written on this very interesting subject, there are none at the popular price of ninepence.

But another good reason for the writing and publication of this one is the fact that it affords a simple guide to the practice of Hypnotism, and an explanation in language easily understood, of a subject that is generally treated far too technically. The present writer has himself experimented in Mesmerism and Hypnotism, so that the reader is assured of practical help.

Use has been made in the preparation of this little work of material from the works of Heidenhain, Bramwell, Coates and Lawrence, and acknowledgments are tendered accordingly to the authors. Readers who require a more

STEPHEN MARTIN

extended survey of the subject might refer to some of the books mentioned in the bibliography on page viii of this work. These can be obtained at the prices quoted from the publishers of "Hypnotism Simplified."

CHAPTER I
WHAT HYPNOTISM IS

UNTIL quite recently there have been two very decided opinions about Hypnotism and Mesmerism in the popular mind. One was that Hypnotism was just quackery, used by knaves to impose upon fools. The other opinion was that Hypnotism and Mesmerism were inventions of the Devil and had best be left severely alone.

Now it is perhaps almost unnecessary to say that both these opinions were wrong. Hypnotism is neither quackery nor the art of the Devil applied by human means.

Hypnotism, as a label, a term, comes from the Greek word "hypnos" sleep. And this is just, in a word, what it means. sleep. But it is a sleep of a particularly wonderful sort, allowing hitherto unknown powers of the mind or soul to become apparent. These powers of the mind are varied and usually become evident in a definite order. Each corresponds to a particular stage of the hypnotic sleep, and the subject passes easily from one stage to the other after becoming influenced by the operator.

It is not proposed here to mystify the reader by a long scientific dissertation. But some reference to the scientific reasons which underlie Hypnotism and Mesmerism will make what follows the easier to grasp.

It is a matter of common knowledge that the old distinction of man, as a trinity of body, soul, and spirit, is beginning to be recognised as true in. science. For a long time the materialistic theory was that man was merely a physical mass that dissipated at death into the chemical elements.

But even the materialist was compelled to distinguish between the mass of the body, the matter and its movements, and the forces that caused them. He had to admit of the existence of energy as well as of that of matter. Then he began to see that in addition to the physical movements of the body there were mental movements, reflections of the mind or ideas, as well as feelings and sensations.

If for that mysterious something that science calls energy we substitute the term spirit, and for that entity, or consciousness, the part of man that thinks, reflects, idealises, and judges or wills, we substitute the term mind or soul, we shall have the trinity of man complete.

Now the body of man is undoubtedly the servant of his mind or soul. Man thinks first and then he acts. Every action is at first a thought or an impulse of some kind. It is, therefore, true to say that as a man thinks so he becomes. We take advantage of this by holding up as examples to our young people ideals of what we wish them to become. We do this because we know that if they think aright they will act aright.

Psychology is the study of these mind processes and reactions to impulses or suggestions. The study of psychology takes into account not only our waking states of consciousness, but also dreaming and other kinds of mental conditions. One of the first axioms of philosophy, which is the science of sciences, is that "That which is not cannot act." Now, we know that in dreaming we certainly think and feel that we are doing things, even if we do not do them in what we call actuality.

No one doubts that in dreaming he is doing something that is, dreaming; and the fact of dreaming establishes not only the existence of the mind as something which we may think about as acting independently of the body at times, but it also establishes the fact that the mind possesses powers which the body does not. As an example we may instance the limitations of time and space. For the body. to get from one point to another in space takes time. The greater the distance the longer is the time occupied.

In dreaming space does not seem to exist for the mind. It traverses distance as though it were not appreciable. Now, the body also knows only one direction in time it passes steadily forward or onward through the present. The body ages steadily. It cannot go backward. It cannot get younger. It cannot get to the future suddenly. It is always acting in the present.

Here, again, . the mind is different. Time does not exist for it in this manner. The mind can go back in time. It can go forward as far as it desires. The mind is not limited to the present. It is free to travel, at a jump, into the future or into the past. As a matter of fact, the mind is constantly doing this. It is continually referring to and reflecting on all the time that has passed. And it is also constantly idealising about the future and future states of mind and body.

Science admits that all this mental action is due to impulses or stimuli from the outside. Our ideas are the result of certain external activities producing in us certain states of mind or feelings. The feelings are the result of sensations caused by impacts from outside. Another thing that science in psychical research admits is the action of mind upon mind in telepathy. This has been called, in simpler language, thought transference.

That the thought of one individual can affect another may appear strange. It may even seem to be impossible. But yet we know from a great number of experiments that ordinary persons in their ordinary consciousness may be so affected by the thought of another. This fact is, in a measure, the basis of Hypnotism. For both in Hypnotism and Mesmerism it is the thought of the operator in *suggestion* that begins the train of the wonderful effects that may be witnessed.

But Hypnotism and Mesmerism offer much more than the mere imposition of the will of one person upon that of another. In the higher phases of Hypnotism the powers of the mind the subconscious mind are exhibited. But first we must make clear what is meant by the subconscious mind.

In addition to its admission of the reality of the soul or mind in man, science now agrees to accept a subdivision of the mind into two distinct phases of activity. The first is the ordinary, normal, or waking mind consciousness. The second phase is that of the mind that does not often come into contact directly with the outer world. It is called, as was said, the subconscious mind, or the subliminal consciousness.

It would seem as though there were a second or higher set of apparatus in the brain for registering all the impressions that it receives, and storing these in case they may be required at some time, whilst the ordinary consciousness is concerned only with the more dominant impressions, and even these fade as newer ones come to replace them. It has been said that the subconscious mind never forgets.

But much more than this, the subconscious mind seems to be in touch with much larger issues than the ordinary consciousness. It seems to possess distinctive and singular powers of exercising judgments not based on logical deduction but accepted as final. It seems also able to function at a distance from the body to see and hear things at great distances. It is also able to see into the future, and to look back into and reconstruct the past.

Now, Hypnotism brings into activity these powers and makes them accessible at the desire of the operator. They are usually exercised, too, without the subject's awareness of them. That is, when the subject sees, in clairvoyance, what is going on at a distance, and describes this in detail to the operator, the subject himself, when restored to normal consciousness, knows nothing of what has happened.

For the time being the subject is, as it were, an extension of the mind of the operator, thinking as he wishes, seeing what he desires to see, or to be seen; hearing what he wishes to hear, or what he wishes to be heard; providing the operator with a new and unique set of senses of wonderful power.

Mesmerism has been referred to above more than once. This, like Hypnotism, is just a label for a set of similar phenomena, which are produced in a somewhat different manner, however. Mesmerism takes its name from the notorious Doctor Mesmer, who, in Paris more than a century ago, became famous for his wonderful powers. His theories were rejected at the time of their presentation (1784), but since then the validity of his powers have been reestablished.

Two things may be noted that are of importance. Science recognises that Hypnotism is merely an abnormal condition which is produced by an unharmful physiological strain of different kinds. Its immediate result is a condition of sleep, deeper in its character than ordinary sleep, and accompanied by catalepsy that is, deathlike rigidity of the limbs and anresthesia.

The other important thing to note is that Hypnotism may be practised by a skilled operator without danger to the subject, if proper precautions be taken.

It is as well here to emphasise the latter point. The operator should be skilled. He should know the subject from A to Z before he begins to experiment.

STEPHEN MARTIN

CHAPTER II
WHAT IT DOES

IN the previous chapter some slight indications were given of what might be expected from the hypnotised or mesmerised subject. In this chapter we propose to deal more in detail with the phenomena, but still in general terms. Then each well marked phase of the phenomena will be treated separately. Practical directions will then be given for the production of the various states.

This line of treatment has been well considered. It is thought to be of more importance first to define the states and their sequence and then to follow on with the instructions how to produce them, so that the experimenter may have a grip of the subject, however slightly, in its completeness before he begins, rather than to give instructions first which the novice might attempt to practise.

HYPNOTISM SIMPLIFIED

Some of the stages in Hypnotism are not particularly well marked, and some subjects pass easily and without very definite indications from one to another. And it might place an operator in a difficulty if he found his subject getting beyond control. The present writer had an experience of this kind. From this he learned the lesson that it is well to be *au fait* with the subject as a whole before beginning experiments. It was another illustration of the danger of a little knowledge.

Initially, Hypnotism or Mesmerism produces in the subject operated upon an artificial sleep of greater intensity or degree, rest, or unconsciousness than normal sleep. Yet the hypnotised subject may be awakened by the mere thought suggestion of the operator. The hypnotic sleep is much deeper than ordinary sleep and seems to produce a much greater relaxation of the nervous and muscular systems. A subject who is extremely tired or fatigued physically, or nervously excited or nervously worn, may be awakened quite fresh after a few minutes' hypnotic sleep. One knows how a change of position, from standing upright, say, to a reclining position, will ease, almost instantaneously, the tired physical system. One remembers how delightful is the feeling of relief to the nerves after sleep for an hour or so. This is mainly because of the complete change of condition.

In Hypnotism it would seem that the rate of change of state is immensely accelerated. If we think of two different individuals we shall find that whereas one may take quite a long time to apprehend an argument, or to take a new viewpoint, the other will see it almost at first glance. The difference between those two individuals illustrates the difference between Hypnotism and ordinary sleep.

But there is more in it than just the time period. There is the intention, the suggestion of the operator that this change shall take place. It is this that shortens the time, or accelerates the pace.

A subject may have a nervous headache or a toothache, for example. As soon as he is hypnotised it is suggested to him that his headache or toothache has gone. And it has. But if the subject is quite normal, that is, if he feels no pain in his waking state it may be suggested to him when hypnotised that he has headache or toothache, and he will immediately feel the pain.

Now, the explanation of this is that nearly all pain is mental. We feel pain in the mind. Feeling is different to sensation; the body has the sensation, the mind transmutes it into feeling. If, therefore, to the mind is given the feeling of pain, the body responds to that suggestion. We may illustrate that in this way. If a person of an affectionate disposition is told that he has lost a near relative he immediately feels great grief. And this is so even if he has not lost the relative, whether the news be true or not.

Sensation and feeling are reflex. The sensation produces the feeling. The feeling produces the sensation. If one is angered, feels anger, he places his body into a particular position more or less unconsciously. In Hypnotism, if the body is placed in a position which it would assume when the individual was angry he will become so.

A problem that is sometimes argued in psychology is, "Does one cry because one feels grief?" or "Does one feel grief because one cries?" Our usual experience m the higher emotions or feelings is that the mental change of state precedes the physical effect. One hears the news, feels grief, and then cries.

Great actresses of strong emotional powers shed real tears. They feel the parts they act so strongly that the feeling necessarily gives rise to the physical effect. It must be evident, then, that if it is possible for one to give the feeling the physical result will follow. In the case of the actress the feeling is produced by herself. In the case of the hypnotised subject the feeling is produced by the operator.

Now, if one does not think of the person who gives us news as reliable and trustworthy the news itself does not worry us. If we are told by a quite unreliable individual that we have lost a relative we feel little consternation or grief. We have to feel first of all that the news is true before it moves us.

This is the case with the hypnotised subject. Unless he trusts in the operator's power to produce effects there will be little result worth speaking about. It is almost a *sine qua non*, a condition precedent, that the mind of the subject shall be impressionable. This is mainly the case only for the earlier stages of hypnosis. For once the hypnotic sleep is produced the subject becomes very amenable to the will of the operator.

Reference was made above to the subject losing the feeling of pain, or the feeling of pain being imposed upon him. This opens up at once the whole question of curative and anresthetic Hypnotism. If the feeling of pain can be removed by suggestion, it must be obvious that pain may be inflicted by sensation which is not felt. A limb may be removed, a cut inflicted, or any lesser injury inflicted with the patient being conscious of it at the time.

Curative Hypnotism is the basis of Christian Science practice, which is either Hypnotism by another operator, or self-Hypnotism. Amesthetic Hypnotism, for conducting operations, is used extensively abroad.

As a matter of fact, nearly all good physicians use, consciously or unconsciously, Hypnotism in their treatment. The doctor who gets the best results is the optimist who insists, cheerfully, that the patient is already better. He brings with him into the sick chamber so strong an aura of health and power that the patient responds at once to his suggestion, and is better.

The word "aura," perhaps, require some explanation. Although not generally admitted by scientists some of them, quite eminent scientists, too; do admit it every individual possesses a radiation from his body of this impalpable material which is closely related to the etheric body.

Clairvoyants can see this etheric body a thin, filmy substance which extends all round and within the physical body. It is, roughly, egg-shaped, and extends, perhaps, to twice or three times the diameter of the physical body. The aura shoots rays of light of various colours through this etheric mass.

The colours represent the rates of vibration of the etheric body and the impulses of feeling, of emotions, or of thought, from moment to moment, as the will sways them in this direction or the other. It is considered to be the potent influences of this nervous aura which are the cause of those instinctive likes and dislikes which animate us from time to time.

It is the aura, too, which is used in Mesmerism to produce the same phenomena by psychic action as are produced in Hypnotism by physiological action. It is the case of the mind influencing the body, instead of the. body influencing the mind. To put a familiar example: if the body becomes fatigued, the powers of the mind respond to this fatigue and become less and less active. Drowsiness overclouds the brain and the mind ceases to operate normally.

On the other hand, if the mind be powerfully stimulated it will react upon the body. A man may be immensely fatigued, too tired to move, too drowsy to think. His mind may be almost a blank. Now, let someone suddenly say to him, "Your child's life is in danger, you can save her!" and the mind is at once stimulated, galvanised into action. The body loses its sense of fatigue. It responds at once to the call made upon it.

It is here we see the possibilities of Hypnotism, the exercise of mind control over the body of another. Pain may be removed, or pain may be inflicted. An action may be arrested, or an action may be initiated and continued almost indefinitely at the word of command. The subject may have his personality changed. He may be made to think he is a child or a woman, and he will act accordingly.

In all these phases he is the mere instrument under the control of the operator. If he is told that a paper bag is an explosive bomb he will handle it as such. If he is told it will explode, he will both see and hear the explosion. If he is told a paperknife is a dangerous weapon, he will treat it as such. In other words, he will see and hear just what is suggested to him. He will do just what he is told without questioning either its relevance, its necessity, or its justice.

But in the higher hypnotic phases the subject becomes more than a mere machine, subject to the behest of the operator. He becomes a person possessed of extremely wide and wonderful powers, capable of seeing things at a distance, of recovering past events, of detecting things hidden, of reading unseen words, etc.

This may be thought to be stretching the longbow, but there is a very large bibliography of the subject, and well authenticated experiments in thousands of cases vouch for the accuracy of the statements above. Many explanations are offered. And most of them tend to prove the existence of powers latent in men.

that were not thought possible to researchers till they had practical proof of them.

CH APTER III
SUGGESTIBILITY

A WORD that has been much abused by those who have written without too much exact knowledge of the subject of Hypnotism is the one that stands at the head of this chapter. These writers say that even the higher phases of Hypnotism are merely examples of suggestibility; that the subject's somnambulance and lucidity are the direct results and that only of the operator's suggestions.

This would imply that the hypnotised subject is limited in his observations and experiences to the contents of the operator's mind; that he cannot see or hear anything which is not directly suggested to him. Later chapters will prove the fallacy of this proposition. It is hoped to establish the fact that subjects have seen and heard things that were unknown to the operator.

What, then, is meant here by the term "suggestibility"? For the bare statement that the human mind is suggestible does not help us very much. We referred before to the fact that if bad news is given the hearer is moved to grief even if the news be found ultimately to be false. From this we may generalise and say that the mind continually acts upon impressions that it receives from the outside. The mind, in fact, is nothing more than the essence of impressions and reactions to them, strung together, as it were, on a thread.

These impressions are received normally through the avenues of the senses in the first place. Then there arise afterimages, as we reflect upon those impressions. An association of ideas follows. And we dissect and analyse them, compare and classify them. These are all mental processes. And the mind is constantly at work upon one or other of them.

Our sensations are constantly being added to our experience is ever definitely widening. We continually receive impressions, and these, by association with other ideas and experience, afterimages and reflections, suggest new combinations. We evolve suggestions from the matrix of mental impressions, and give them to other minds by the exercise of speech, and, more subtly still, by thought waves. We receive suggestions from other minds by the same methods.

This book is a practical example. The writer is suggesting certain things. The reader is receiving them--or some of them. The writer has himself received those suggestions he is now making, either as the result of actual sensory impressions, from reflections of what he has seen and heard, or from experiments he has made.

Let us get back to illustrations again. The thought of appetising food will suggest hunger. The thought of a restful couch or chair will suggest repose, and incline one to feel sufficiently fatigued to desire rest. And this is true whether we originate the thought that is, if it appeals to us directly or if it is suggested by someone else.

25

All our lives we are acting thus upon suggestions received from outside though many of them we believe to originate in ourselves. From infancy right through childhood suggestion is playing its part in moulding our lives. Education and parental training is almost wholly suggestive.

To say, then, that the human mind is suggestible is to convey all these points thus raised above.

Now, in Hypnotism the tendency to act immediately upon suggestion is almost irresistible. In normal waking life we have the reasoning powers to check our tendency to act upon suggestions. But in the hypnotic condition the normal mental powers of reflection, association of ideas, and reasoning are inhibited the subject is much more susceptible to suggestion. He is highly suggestible.

We find in some normal persons remarkable instances of the power of suggestion. They have read cleverly worded descriptions of symptoms of diseases. And immediately they begin to feel those symptoms themselves. In time they actually do suffer and exhibit those symptoms.

When, therefore, the operator in hypnosis makes a suggestion to his subject the latter is mainly influenced by this suggestion because he has reason to believe that what the operator suggests is true. If the operator says to him, "I want you to look steadily at this disc, or little mirror, for a few minutes. You will probably become drowsy. Make no attempt to resist this. If you want to sleep, do so. Close your eyes when I tell you, etc.," a whole train of suggestion is given and predisposes the subject to accept and act upon all other suggestions given by the operator.

In Hypnotism this suggestibility of the human mind is used initially to secure the artificial sleep of the subject which is accompanied by his increasing willingness to accept all suggestions made to him. In Mesmerism the same effect is produced by a continued gaze from the operator and the exercise of his magnetic force upon the subject.

Really all Hypnotism employs mesmeric methods, because the very fact that the operator believes in his power to produce hypnosis by physiological strain of some sort disposes him to act magnetically and mesmerically. He also concentrates his gaze and his will. His aura, too, is making radiations and influencing his subject.

It was said above that the suggestibility of the subject increases enormously as soon as he begins to come under the power of the operator. At first the subject may resist almost unconsciously. He may be willing to accept the suggestion, but feels that it is ridiculous. But if he keeps a passive mind he will realise that keeping still is always the easiest method to induce sleep. Fixing the attention ·on something always assists the process.

In a few minutes, therefore, most individuals will find that the suggestion of drowsiness begins to operate, and they do go off into a pleasant and dreamless sleep, from which they may be awakened easily and refreshed for the repose. The acceptance of the suggestion to sleep when once acted upon by the subject at the behest of the operator makes subsequent hypnoses easy for both.

Nothing is easier to acquire than a habit. Any action is much more easily accomplished the second time than the first. So that when the operator, on another occasion, tells the subject almost at once to close his eyes and "Sleep," the suggestion is obeyed immediately.

And as soon as the hypnotic sleep itself is apparent the subject becomes more and more suggestible. His power to resist, or to reason about any suggestion made to him, or command given to him, disappears and he is quite under control by the operator.

CHAPTER IV
CREDULITY

THIS stage in hypnotic phenomena is the inevitable result of the use of the subject's susceptibility to suggestion. Having accepted the operator's suggestion that he should sleep, he is now in the mood to respond vividly and instantaneously to any command given him. From being more or less suggestible he becomes credulous. He believes, accepts orders, and acts just as he is told.

Actually, most of the phenomena of credulity take place when the subject is apparently awakened after the first hypnotic stage has been accomplished. The procedure is to induce the sleep either by passes or a concentrated gaze on the part of the subject. The eyes are then closed by the operator and the subject is told to sleep. Then, by gently blowing upon the face, or in other ways to be detailed later, the subject is restored the use of his sight, but still remains subject to suggestion.

If now he is told to stroke the cat that he is nursing he will do so, and the cat is actually there so far as he is concerned. He can see it, feel its weight and the warmth of its body. If told that he must be careful with the child that he is holding a handkerchief rolled up will do to emphasise the suggestion he will fondle the child which he believes himself to hold.

In this credulous condition most of the simpler phenomena are exhibited. A subject, when told that he cannot move, will find that that is so. An imaginary wall may be pointed out to him and he will be unable to pass the spot it occupies. If told that a piece of raw potato, for example, is a peach he will eat it and derive all the accustomed flavour and pleasurable sensations of taste from it.

A great delicacy, a sweetmeat, for example, may be given him to eat, but when told that it is something disagreeable he believes the statement implicitly and has experience of great disgust. From these examples it will be seen how much the subject is under the control of the operator.

In this condition, a suggestion given will be acted upon later. For instance, if told that when the operator counts six he is to perform some certain action the subject will continue to do as is suggested to him until the operator counts loudly one-two-three-four-five-six, when, at once, he ceases what he is doing and performs the action previously suggested.

Imitative phenomena is a phase of the credulous condition. The operator will say, "Place your hands thus. Now, do as I do," and he revolves one hand round the other. Then to the subject, who follows his movements, he will say, "Faster, faster!" and find that it is done. Then he may say, "You cannot stop. You must go on," and the subject is compelled to do so, even to the point of exhaustion.

But when told emphatically by the operator, "Stop!" he does so. Any other similar action or series of actions may be thus initiated, and will be continued by the subject, automatically, if he is told that he cannot stop. The imitation is the beginning of the action; the suggestion that the subject cannot stop makes it automatic. From what has been said before it will be perceived that this phase of Hypnotism does not exhibit any of the higher powers of the inner mind. In fact, it does just the reverse. It leaves the subject very much at the behest of the operator. Within reasonable limits anything that he may be told to do he will do, or endeavour to do.

Because of this, however, this phase of Hypnotism is very valuable for curative purposes. The subject, being almost wholly dependent upon the suggestions of the operator, and believing in them implicitly, may be treated accordingly. If he is told, for example, that some little habit of his is objectionable, that he ought not to do it, that he will find it easy now not to do it; in fact, it will be almost impossible for him to do it, this will affect him considerably in the normal waking state and tend to break down the habit.

STEPHEN MARTIN

This little book is not intended, however, to be a treatise on curative Hypnotism. Those who wish to use the science curatively are recommended to read some of the larger works to which reference has been made in the preface. Simple little experiments like removing a headache, by inducing sleep and then suggesting that the patient will wake in a few minutes refreshed and with all pain gone, may be done, but little beyond this without due care and thorough preparation by reading the more important books on the subject.

Much innocent amusement may be had, and without risk, if the operator is satisfied with the earlier phases of Hypnotism and does not attempt anything ambitious. Imitative automatism and the other phenomena of the credulous stage ought to satisfy the beginner for some time. When he feels himself quite proficient with this stage, and with many different subjects, it will be quite time to attempt something more showy.

Then by easy stages he may pass along to experiments in the higher phases of Hypnotism and Mesmerism, if he can find suitable subjects. For it must be said here that although nearly everyone is susceptible to the earlier, or simpler, phases of Hypnotism, there are not nearly so many who exhibit the higher phases of somnambulance and lucidity.

CHAPTER V
LETHARGY AND CATALEPSY

IN the last chapter some of the phenomena of the credulous stage were described, and it was said that in this the subject was apparently awakened and his vision restored to him by his eyes being opened. It was seen, however, that he could only see what he was told to see, and saw also things that were not really there. Actually, therefore, he was still hypnotised, although to an audience he looked as though he were really awake.

If instead of being thus aroused the subject is allowed to continue to sleep, and the suggestion given to him that his sleep is deep and sound" You are fast asleep. Very soundly asleep," the operator says the subject passes steadily into most profound torpor or lethargy. In this condition the subject would remain, perhaps, for twenty-four hours or longer, if not told to wake earlier. The lethargic condition closely resembles that of ordinary, profound sleep, but it is impossible, except hypnotically, to rouse the subject. He may be rolled about like a sack of wheat, or slapped and banged, without result.

The operator can, however, recall his subject to the lighter phases by making suitable suggestions to him. "You will wake in five minutes. You are not sleeping so heavily now. Your sleep is getting lighter and lighter. I can wake you now if I wish. The five minutes is passing. It is nearly up. You will wake very soon now. Wake!" This will be detailed more fully in its proper chapter.

There is not much interesting phenomena from the lethargic stage, but it is useful in curative Mesmerism to secure a long sleep for a patient who needs continued physical repose and rest from nerve strain. For the ordinary performer there is little attraction in this phase except for its close connection with the much more extraordinary one of catalepsy.

In catalepsy most of the phenomena of death are produced. There is a stiffening of all the limbs until complete rigidity of the whole body is obtained, a lower beat of the heart is to be observed, and the breathing is very much reduced. Not all subjects pass into the complete cataleptic condition.

It is usual to produce rigidity of one or other of the limbs hypnotically by stroking nerves and nerve centres, and mesmerically by passes over the same areas. The subject is told to extend an arm, say. Then the operator, making passes from the body outward, or by stroking the limb, suggests also to the subject that the limb is becoming rigid. "It will not bend. It is getting stiffer and stiffer, etc." And the subject finds he is really unable to bend the limb.

This cataleptic condition can be simulated, so far as the subject himself is concerned, in the credulous stage by telling him that his arm is stiff and he cannot bend it. But the operator could bend it at the joints though the subject

himself is unable to do so. In the real cataleptic condition rigidity is produced in reality, and neither the operator nor anyone else, without breaking bones, or lacerating tendons and muscles, could bend the arm.

What actually happens is that the muscles and nerves are paralysed into inaction. By placing the subject's arms close to his side and then catalepsing these, and then the legs, and finally the whole body, he resembles then an upright log. If pushed he will topple over forwards or backwards without a bone or muscle moving.

A thoroughly catalepsed subject may be placed with his feet upon the back of one chair and his neck resting upon the back of another, and his rigid body will then support the weight of several persons. This used to be a favourite experiment with professional public performers, and at first trickery was suspected.

But medical men who have studied the science of Hypnotism have seen that there is no trickery in this. It is just the application of ordinary natural law by inducing a physiological strain. If the nerves are paralysed the muscles will not act they cannot act, in fact. And this condition of nervous inaction is produced quite simply by stroking the nerve channels.

In catalepsy the subject feels no pain. It is as though an anresthetic of the freezing variety had been used. A catalepsy subject. may be pricked with a needle, a needle has been passed right through the hand of a subject without his feeling it. A somewhat similar condition to the cataleptic lethargic one is that used for operations by surgeons. The patient then is quite quiet there is no reflex action of the body, and no pain is felt.

From the cataleptic condition the subject is restored by reversing the process that produced the catalepsy. Upward passes or strokings are made, accompanied by the suggestion that the limbs and body are becoming less rigid, and finally commanding the subject to move his limbs and trunk.

No word of caution should be needed here to show the novice that he should not venture into this deep water until he knows he can swim in the shallows by repeated simpler experiments.

CHAPTER VI
SOMNAMBULANCE

As hinted before, this is a phase of Hypnotism that is not very frequently exhibited. Experimenters must not be disappointed, therefore, if they fail to obtain phenomena of this character from an otherwise suitable medium, or subject.

Some writers on Hypnotism and Mesmerism treat somnambulance and lucidity, or clairvoyance, as though the two stages were the same. Although the present writer regards them as very closely allied, he prefers to treat them rather as distinct phases, the somnambulistic leading almost directly to the still higher phase of lucidity.

If we think of ordinary sleep walking we shall realise what is meant by the expression in Hypnotism, having in view the possibility of the astral or etheric double possessing the power, as a thought vehicle, or passing freely through space whilst the physical body of the subject remains in the presence of the operator.

It may appear to be a wide claim to make for it that a subject should be able to project his consciousness to another part of the world and to see and hear what is going on there. Yet this is what somnambulism means in this connection. Evidence is available in the larger books on the subject that this is the most reasonable hypothesis to explain the phenomena actually obtained.

It has been suggested that the best method of awakening this power is to direct the attention of the subject to some distant place, which he knows well, and to ask him to transfer his consciousness thereto see what is occurring. At first the process is assisted by suggestion. And ordinarily it is led up to by easy steps.

With the eyes of the subject closed, he is asked to read a letter which is visible to the operator. Here undoubtedly telepathy, or thought transference, assists. Then the subject is led on to try to see something in another room which the operator knows to be there. The subject is asked to describe it in detail. Then, perhaps, he is asked to say who put it there, or who handled it last, and so on.

In this way he is gradually reduced to use a new set of organs and a vehicle for his consciousness which is possibly that normally used in the dreaming state. Ordinary somnambulance arises from the patient visiting scenes with his physical body. In hypnotic somnambulance the physical body is entranced rendered incapable of locomotion and the astral double, or etheric vehicle, is then the seat of consciousness and travels freely through space.

Apparitions of the dead and dying are to be attributed to this possibility of the etheric double travelling freely through space whilst the physical body. is almost inert and the connection between them reduced to a minimum.

It must be remembered that Hypnotism and Mesmerism depend almost wholly upon this capacity of using the psychic senses and the psychic body, or etheric astral vehicle. A *sine qud non* is the repose of the physical body, brought about in the first place by 'the hypnotic sleep.

It will be seen from the above that not only is this power of somnambulance comparatively rare in subjects, but also that it must not be expected. to be manifested at once. The subject has to be trained and exercised in the use of these higher faculties. He is, for the nonce, somewhat like an infant, struggling to attain articulate expression and gradually acquiring powers of locomotion.

The operator who desires to get results of the higher type, therefore, must not be discouraged because he fails after several efforts. If he really desires to succeed he must try again and again with the same subject, and only when quite satisfied that results are not to be obtained should he go on to another subject and begin again the series of trials. Usually it will be found in time that a suitable subject is forthcoming, and that gradually a gleam of success is achieved.

Lucidity is the more general term for powers of clairvoyance and clairaudience. The subject here is not only free of the limitation of space, but also of those of time. Past, present, and future are all one to him. He sees everything as the present. It is as though the spark of intuitive faculty, of which we all sometimes have evidence, begins to blossom in the subject and rapidly attains a full measure of growth.

Then the subject is able to see and hear not only what is transpiring near and far, but also what has happened, and what is going to happen. If one is asked for an explanation of how this is, all that can be suggested is that in the hypnotic condition in the most ordinary subjects all the senses seem to be most preternaturally acute. The sense of taste and sense of smell and of hearing are wonderfully sharpened. And this appears to be, from evidence adduced, independently of suggestion.

If this is so in the earlier phases, what may not be expected in the deeper phases of hypnosis when the astral vehicle is freed almost entirely from its connection with the physical body and comes into possession of a most exalted and extended set of senses or faculties?

Dr. Coates says of clairvoyance, in his "Human Magnetism," that the subject "*sees* --or, perhaps, to be more correct, *perceives*--or becomes in some subtle way cognisant of the existence of objects and persons --living and discarnate--their thoughts, desires, emotions, and other states of mind, under circumstances which preclude deductions made per physical vision, and in which physical vision is impossible. The history of Mesmerism teems with such cases, to say nothing of psychological medicine and modern spiritualism, while recent hypnotic practice has conceded a 'supernormal power of vision,' discernible under hypnosis. But whether Professor Gregory's explanation of the phenomenon be acceptable to modern experts or not, that is another question.

STEPHEN MARTIN

Clairvoyance is now practically conceded, and that is everything. How a clairvoyant sees or perceives must in our present knowledge be a matter for investigation, as many other subjects in life are. Mesmeric and magnetic phenomena establish the fact that he does see in some supernormal way, while a survey of many peculiar pathological cases proves the possibility of man seeing independently of what we call sight. And we have now and then remarkable cases of totally blind persons being able to *see* clairvoyantly. It is true that some clairvoyants speak of seeing, and others of feeling and of being impressed. These modes of expression do not amount to much, when we take into consideration that the information given of scenes, events, and incidents, beyond the range of human vision, is a remarkable proof, and where not so an acknowledgment, of man's complex nature, or 'other consciousness.'

"The human body has been explored again and again with marked accuracy and correctness in diagnosis by mesmeric and by normal clairvoyants. In many cases clairvoyance has proved and may still prove to be an invaluable agent in the diagnosis of disease. Some subjects are much more lucid, more graphic and connected in their descriptions than others, so much depending on the temperament, the education or the practice of the clairvoyant, and the presence and influence of a good operator at the start, some experimenters being wholly incapable of inducing somnambulistic lucidity, as they have never been able to get beyond that objective suggestion stage of hypnotic experimentation, now so popular with medical hypnotic practitioners.

"In the lucid somnambulistic state, subjects have the power of sensing or perceiving certain very fine or subtle impressions conveyed by all objects to the sensorium by the medium of some agent or 'influence,' which has been called by mesmerists 'Magnetic Fluid,' or 'Vital Magnetism; by Reichenbach 'Octyle,' and by theosophists 'Astral Light,' and indeed, so far as my own experiments have gone, I am convinced that clairvoyants perceive that which is seen by a light emanating from and peculiar to the object or persons described, and not to any ordinary light vibrations stimulating the vision centres, per the eye or in any other way. It matters little whether the clairvoyant sees with closed eyes, as is usually the case, or with open eyes, that which is perceived being in all cases beyond the range of ordinary vision. In fact, the clairvoyant can see what persons awake and in normal conditions cannot see. Usually the impressions or vibrating stimuli conveyed to the clairvoyant would be wholly overpowered by the more intrusiveimpressions received through the activity of the sense organs.

Hypnosis helps to cut off these coarser impressions and permits the greater play of subconscious or psychic faculty of perception, which is clairvoyance. When clairvoyance manifests in the waking state, as it frequently does, under apparently normal conditions in some persons, it only does so while they are in a state of reverie, abstraction, in which the coarser sense impressions are cut off as they are in absentmindedness. The condition has been consciously induced by *vague contemplation* by Eastern adepts, and unconsciously by many persons, nearer home, through that dreamy contemplation peculiar to the borderland between the waking and sleeping states overtaking many in passive thought conditions which notably precede, in the history of clairvoyance, all spontaneous impressions and visions, symbolical, or clear, vivid and direct.

"Some clairvoyants are able to see through opaque substances, as well as into the human body; they are capable of analysing the mental conditions of persons, near or far removed, with whom they come in *rapport*, and whom they examine through their psychic telescopes for the time being.

"Many clairvoyants are clairaudient too, and hear sounds and voices which cannot be heard by ordinary sense organs. These peculiar conditions have not been unknown to mesmerists in the past. And now that these facts are accepted by men of science; I think the most bigoted hypnotist will have to recognise that in this, as in clairvoyants, the much despised mesmerist was right, too.'"

Of this very interesting phase of Hypnotism, Dr. Gregory says: '"The clairvoyant sees with the internal cerebral vision, but not by means of ordinary light, which is excluded by the shut eye and other circumstances, such as an intervening wall.

'"We can easily suppose the sensations of form, light, and colour to be excited in the internal seat of vision by other means than ordinary light, for we know that these may be excited in the dark by pressure on the eyeball or by congestion of the vessels of the eye, or by other more obscure means."

Some hypnotists and writers on Hypnotism do not admit the explanations given above; in fact, they prefer to reject the idea altogether of clairvoyance. They admit readily enough the evidence compels them to do this, that the subject sees things at a distance, but prefer to maintain that when such is the case it is no more than telepathy, and that, unconsciously perhaps, some other individual has transmitted the thoughts so strongly that they have become apparent the senders themselves to the subject. But then telepathy is surely as wonderful as clairvoyance. And, after all, the main point is that the subject does see, or becomes cognisant of, what is happening elsewhere.

There is a consensus of opinion on the part of all writers on Hypnotism against inexperienced persons trying to hypnotise others without knowing exactly what to do. Frequently it happens that hypnosis easily occurs, and then the amateur operator becomes excited or puzzled and does not know what to do. The subject then becomes unduly excited also, and some nervous trouble may ensue.

It is for this reason that we have delayed giving practical directions for even the elementary stages till some idea of the whole subject has first been presented.

STEPHEN MARTIN

CHAPTER VII
PRACTICAL DIRECTIONS

IT will have been gathered from the foregoing chapters that there are at least two distinct methods of inducing the sleep or trance condition in hypnosis: the one by psychic means, fascination of the gaze, radiations from the aura, and passes, and the other by physiological means, eye ·or ear strain, and strokings or touches on nerve centres or areas.

As a matter of fact, the psychic processes, the mesmeric or magnetic, depend upon physiological reactions in the body of the subject, and the physiological processes, the hypnotic, depend upon mental or psychic help from suggestion. Both are roads that lead to the same goal, and both really are dual in nature: the psychical and physical are so closely bound together, interwoven, one might say, that what affects one necessarily secures reaction, or reflex, in the other.

STEPHEN MARTIN

The operator, then, is able to make use of either method; or he may, for preference, combine the two that is, use a physiological strain, but accompany it with magnetic or mesmeric passes. The combined method, in the opinion of the present writer, is the easiest method to obtain control.

It goes without saying that the subject should be willing to try. It is possible to hypnotise one against his will, but it simplifies matters immensely if the subject is willing to be operated upon. The fact that he is willing to adapt himself to the preliminary requirements of the operator provides the first link in the chain of suggestibility, credulity I and automatism, etc.

Generally, I it is believed that weak minded individuals make the best subjects. But this is not true. Almost everyone can be hypnotised. Some individuals, however I respond much more readily than others.

Coates and many others give detailed instructions for testing the susceptibility without actual hypnosis. But there is scarcely any need to go into this. A few hints instead will enable the novice operator to test practically the capacity of his subject.

But first of all, it is necessary that he should have no doubt in his own mind of what he is going to do. He must be convinced, firstly, that it can be done; and, secondly I that he can do it. His will must be concentrated upon the matter in hand. It is useless for him to try if he feels that it may be a failure, or that, for instance, he is just making a fool of himself.

He must keep his mind firmly fixed upon the course he proposes to pursue. Any vacillation on his part, any indecision, any faltering or lack of confidence, will inevitably be reflected in the behaviour of his subject. On the other hand, his self-confidence and belief in his power to accomplish what he says he is going to do will be the first step in establishing control. If the subject trusts him he becomes almost immediately suggestible.

STEPHEN MARTIN

The operator's first desire is to get his subject to sleep. This, then, is the point upon which his own mind must be fixed. All that he does or says must be in the direction of achieving that purpose. He must instill into the subject's mind that he has the power to do this, and is going to do it. The thought currents which emanate from the operator will affect his subject. If the operator wavers in his concentration the subject is affected thereby.

Concentration and "willing'" on the part of the operator occasions the passing from him to the subject of nerve-auric currents or radiations- -or magnetic waves, as some prefer to call them. These react upon the subject mentally, first of all, and then affect him physiologically.

Having now got himself well under control, the operator should place his subject comfortably in a chair. The subject should face the light. It will assist both operator and subject if the former makes commands, as it were, of everything he wishes done. "You must sit here, please. Seat yourself comfortably, so that you may rest and sleep. Place your hands so. The elbows must be close to the side, but not pressing against them. Place your feet so and so, etc."

In all this there is much purposive action and suggestion. The subject is already surrendering himself to the suggestion of the operator. The latter is making the way smooth for the more emphatic commands and suggestions which are soon to follow.

Now, the operator may proceed, when his subject is comfortably seated, in many different ways. One of the simplest is to use the disc method. A disc of zinc, with a centre stud of copper, the whole disc to be about the size of a crown piece, is given to the subject to hold in the palm of one hand, which is to rest upon the palm of the other, both on his knees.

"You must fix your gaze upon the centre copper spot," he is told, "and you will find that in a very short time you will feel inclined to sleep. Do not resist that feeling. Allow it to make itse1£ manifest as quickly as it likes. When I tell you to close your eyes, close them." And so on.

Then the operator may proceed to make downward passes. This is done as follows: Standing just in front of the subject, with hands outstretched, palms towards the subject, fingertips upwards, the hands should be drawn down smoothly and easily from just above the head to the chest, or a little lower. The hands of the operator should then be closed and arms extended on either side of the subject to raise the hands away from the body of the subject. Then, just above the head, with fingertips upwards, palms towards the subject, the downward pass should be repeated.

Starting with the palms a few inches from the face, the distance should be gradually decreased, till the pass becomes almost, but not quite, a personal contact all the way.

After a few minutes the operator should, whilst making the passes, use mental as well as verbal suggestions" You are beginning to feel sleepy. Your eyes are tired. You are losing feeling in your legs and your arms. Your body begins to rest. You are going to sleep. You will be sleeping in a minute, etc." He may then cease the passes for a moment and present the tips of his fingers towards the eyes of the subject. If the eyelids tremble and blink, as they will almost certainly do, the operator will say, "Your eyes are closing. You cannot keep them open. You are going to sleep, fast asleep. You are sleeping now. You cannot open your eyesthey are quite fast, etc."

He will find, probably, that the subject now makes some little effort to open his eyes the muscular system around the eyelids betrays this but the subject cannot open his eyes. And when this has been accomplished the first stage is successfully achieved.

Another method of getting the subject to sleep is that of fixing his gaze upon your eyes, while you "will" that he shall sleep, and make verbal and mental suggestion to that effect either without or with passes, after the first minute or two. It assists the hypnosis for the operator to seat himself in front of the subject, and, if he decides to do without passes, to join hands with the subject, pressing gently, but firmly with the balls of his thumbs against those of the subject. This contact may be broken after a few minutes, when the pupils of the subject's eyes begin to expand, and the operator's fingertips are advanced to close the eyes, saying, "Now your eyes are closing. You are going to sleep, fast asleep, etc."

Yet another method is to get the subject to gaze upwards at your extended fingers a few inches above his forehead, and away from it. This produces a slight eye strain which, accompanied by the verbal suggestion, soon results in the hypnotic sleep.

Once the subject has been made to sleep in obedience to suggestion he becomes very amenable to the will and command of the operator. The subject acts readily upon the suggestions made to him. But the novice should never proceed with experiments until he has established completely to his own satisfaction, and to that of his subject, his power to release him from the hypnosis directly he desires to do so.

In this first phase a few upward passes should be made, and then a cold breath, blown into the face of the subject, will bring him round. A mental suggestion should ·be made at the same time, and if thought necessary the verbal command may finally be given, "Wake!" in a firm and confident tone.

A little practice will soon convince the operator that it is quite easy to control his subject. Only one subject, and preferably the same individual, should be tried for a few séances in succession till the operator gains confidence and skill.

Then a little further progress may be made. The lips may be fastened by a verbal suggestion, accompanied by lightly touching the nerve centres at the corners of the mouth, to emphasise the suggestion. The mouth may be firmly closed in similar fashion, and the subject will be unable to open his lips or mouth, or to speak.

Now this may be extended to the limbs. The arms may be fixed to the sides by making passes and suggestions to this effect. The hands can be fixed to the knees. The feet may be glued to the floor. The body fixed firmly in the chair, etc. In every case the final effect is led up to by the verbal suggestions made, and at last the patient is told, "You cannot move. You are quite fixed. Your arms are tied to your body. Your hands are firmly fixed to your knees. Your feet cannot move. Your body is fixed in that chair, etc." These suggestions will be accepted and the subject actually will be unable to move.

As the trials are extended, and the deeper lethargic sleep is approached, cataleptic experiments may be tried. The arm of the subject may be extended straight out from the body. Passes should be made from the body towards the subject's fingertips, and mental and verbal suggestions given--'"Your arm is getting stiff. It is becoming quite rigid. It is now quite stiff. It will remain thus. You cannot move it. It will not bend, etc."

In every case, after each trial, the subject should be restored to the normal condition before further attempts are made to carry the hypnosis a stage farther. The operator must be content for some time with very simple phenomena until he feels absolutely sure of himself. In the meanwhile he should study the more important books to perfect himself in recognising easily the various stages as they affect the other subjects he may now try.

CHAPTER VIII
AWAKENING THE SUBJECT

IT sometimes happens, as was hinted in earlier chapters, that a subject does not respond readily to the more ordinary methods of awakening him. Perhaps he has passed from the simpler first stage of hypnotic sleep into a far deeper phase of lethargy, and the operator is a little puzzled as to what to do.

He must keep his head and not resort to forcible measures. A few additional upward passes may be all that is necessary to bring the subject back to the simpler phase from which he may be awakened by the cold breath, by the command to "Wake!" or by a sharp clapping of the hands in front of the face simultaneously. If the subject fails to respond to this, and seems too heavily asleep to be awakened, the operator should proceed with his verbal suggestions in the following manner: "You are to sleep less heavily. You are to pay attention to what I say. You can hear me. I want you to answer me. You do hear me. You can answer. Now, then, answer! Do you hear me?"

Almost invariably a reply will be given that the subject does hear. Then the operator proceeds: "I want you to wake when I count ten. Will you wake when I count ten?" To this also the answer will most certainly be in the affirmative. And then, after a pause, the operator may proceed to count slowly, "'One, two, three, etc.," and at "ten," uttered sharply and commandingly, he may add, "Wake!"

If a subject proves intractable, as a rule, suggestions should be made to him as soon as the hypnotic sleep is begun that he shall wake in a given time, or at a particular signal, etc. These suggestions should be made confidently, and the subject should be got to acknowledge them" You understand me. You will wake in ten minutes from now. Answer me. Say that you will wake in ten minutes."

It is as well to remember that reversing a process almost necessarily destroys the original effect. The upward passes neutralise the downward passes. But as sometimes the subject actually passes automatically once the sequence has been begun into a deeper phase of hypnosis than the operator intends, it may be necessary to use more frequent upward passes than the downward passes used to produce the hypnosis.

Usually it is considered that the effects of any phase will wear itself out in a few hours. The subject then passes into a normal sleep, from which he may easily be wakened in the ordinary manner. But every care should be taken by the operator to maintain his control over the subject and waken him whenever he desires to do so, unless the purpose of the hypnosis is purely curative, and a long, deep, and restful sleep is to be produced.

By following the principles enunciated above there should be little difficulty in maintaining control of the subject if suggestions are given early to the effect that he must hear and obey all orders given to him by the operator. This is particularly desirable if the higher phases of

Hypnotism are attempted. Control must be maintained so that the séance can be terminated when the operator considers it necessary.

The operator himself must remember that practice alone will fit him to use these powers successfully. And since they involve some considerable strain upon him, in concentration and in intensity of will projection, he should be in good condition, well rested, physically and mentally, before he begins a séance. The séance should not be prolonged. And another should not follow rapidly. There should be time for rest and recuperation between.

CHAPTER IX
SELF-HYPNOTISM

THIS chapter might well be expanded to become a book in itself. But only a few simple hints will be given for the use of self-hypnotism, which may be beneficially employed by everyone.

In an earlier chapter some time was devoted to an explanation of the suggestibility of the mind, and also to the duplex character of the mind. This duplexity of the mind is the basis of self-hypnotism. It is because of the difference of level, as it were, or of potential, in the electrical sense, that Hypnotism may be self -applied.

If the normal mind takes an idea and holds it firmly before itself suggests this idea, in fact, to the subconscious mind the latter entity takes up the work suggested to it in due course. Bad habits can thus be broken. Good ones can thus be instituted.

HYPNOTISM SIMPLIFIED

Nearly all the great and powerful ones of the earth have become so because they have, consciously or unconsciously, used self-hypnotism. In most cases it has been unconscious. Nevertheless it has been self-hypnosis. It has been first the recognition of the desirability of an idea, and next the holding firmly to that idea before the subconscious mind until it has become a power for good or evil.

It may be that wealth was sought. And this mainly for the power it produces to move men and things. Early in their careers these men have seen that an idea can transform their lives, that a thought persisted in means a complete making over of the whole substance of their natures. That idea they have held before themselves, and it has materialised as they wished--as they desired--as they intended.

"As a man thinks so he becomes."' This is profoundly true. To him who desires ardently and "wills" steadfastly nothing is denied. But faith without works is of no avail. And equally true is it that works without faith will avail little.

STEPHEN MARTIN

One has to be convinced first of the truth of this saying, "To will is to have" and then to act upon it. Within man lie powers scarcely dreamed of. He must first recognise that it is within his power to do things, and then all things are possible.

A simple consideration will convince the sceptic of the power and of the activity of the subconscious mind. If it is not within his own experience, let him ask a few of his friends if they use the power of autosuggestion to wake themselves from sleep at a given time. All that it is necessary to do is to impress upon the subconscious mind, just before composing oneself to sleep, that one "wills" to wake at a definite time. The idea of waking must be uttered as a command, as a suggestive order, and it will be obeyed.

This principle can be applied in almost every direction. By choosing a suitable time to meditate upon what one desires to become, and impressing that idea upon the subconscious mind, the difficulties in the way will be smoothed and the path rendered easy to traverse. This is no idle notion. It is the outcome of practical experience. It is just a simple repetition of one of nature's great laws, known, perhaps, to a few only, and practised by still fewer.

Let the reader who desires to put the matter to the test take, first, some little alteration that he desires made in his life or circumstances. Mere idle dreaming of the change will not do. He must "will" strongly. He must act accordingly. By suggesting to himself, first, the desirability of the change next, its possibility; and, finally, his "will" .that it shall be so, he will find his efforts are speedily successful.

It may be that he desires order, or punctuality, or attentiveness to business to result. A strong suggestion to the subconscious mind will make it easy for him to put in force his intention. He will find, however, that every endeavour will meet with opposition. This is the mental reaction of the habitual life. But the suggestion persevered with quickly breaks this down, and conquest follows conquest.

STEPHEN MARTIN

Progress is made step by step. But each step, although greater, is the more easily taken. Nothing succeeds like success. For it is always the first move that is the hardest. It is hard, first of all, to break down the feeling of laissez faire. "It doesn't matter" is the enemy to be beaten first. The recognition of the possibility of success acts like a charm. It is a charm. For its virtue is to arm the bearer with unbeatable weapons.

New thought, higher thought, Christian Science wonders, all depend upon this power of self-suggestion. Much of it is purely ethical training. And ethical training is of immense value even in a commercial world like that of today, ·where sharp practice is at a premium. The man who is eminently straightforward and dependable, whose word may be relied upon absolutely, who keeps faith and time, who holds to a bargain made, who' knows what he wants and does not hesitate to step straight forward to take it, whilst respecting the rights of other she is the man who not only makes way, but gains the respect and esteem of those with whom he comes in contact.

www.ingramcontent.com/pod-product-compliance
Lightning Source LLC
Chambersburg PA
CBHW060256030426
42335CB00014B/1721